Beer

Chips Barber

GW00802207

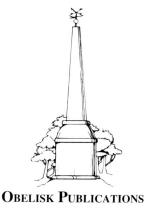

OBELISK PUBLICATIONS

ALSO BY THE AUTHOR

Branscombe
The Story of Dawlish Warren
The Story of Hallsands
Walk the East Devon Coast – Lyme Regis to Lympstone
The Lost City of Exeter – Revisited • The Great Little Exeter Book
The Ghosts of Exeter • Beautiful Exeter
Topsham Past and Present • Sidmouth Past and Present • Honiton Past and Present
Topsham in Colour • Sidmouth in Colour • Exmouth in Colour
Short Circular Walks in and around Sidmouth • Sidmouth of Yesteryear
Along The Otter • Walks on and around Woodbury Common

OTHER BOOKS ABOUT THIS AREA

An Exeter Boyhood, *Frank Retter*
Exploring Exeter–The Heart of the City, *Jean Maun*
Exploring Exeter–The West Quarter, *Jean Maun*
Exploring Exeter–The Quay, *Jean Maun*
Cullompton Past and Present, *Jane Leonard*
Exmouth to Starcross Ferry, *Harry Pascoe*
Strange Stories from Exmouth, *Tricia Gerrish*
Around the Churches of East Devon, *Walter Jacobson*
Curiosities of East Devon, *Derrick Warren*

*We have over 200 Devon-based titles. For a list of current books please send SAE to
2 Church Hill, Pinhoe, Exeter, EX4 9ER. Tel: (01392) 468556.*

ACKNOWLEDGEMENTS

I would like to thank the following for their help: T. Michael Pritchard, Managing Director of Peco, for his help and support, and for the loan of pictures on pages 30 and 31; John Scott and the dedicated team at Beer Quarry Caves for their support and enthusiasm; and Alan Abbott, a Beer stalwart (and excellent Father Christmas!) who kindly supplied the occasional anecdote and the old picture postcard views found on pages 5, 6, 7, 8, 9, 10, 12, 14, 15, 18, 19, 20, 21, 22, 23, 24, 25 and 27.

*First published in 2004 by
Obelisk Publications, 2 Church Hill, Pinhoe, Exeter, Devon
Designed and Typeset by Sally Barber
Printed in Great Britain
Avocet Press, Cullompton, Devon*

Beer

W hat's in a name? Well, here in Devon, the town of Beer has absolutely nothing to do with my favourite drink! As with the other variations of 'bere' and 'beare', it most probably means 'wood', although in the deep depression now occupied by the village any forest has long since gone.

The 1930s produced some whimsical thoughts on the name. Under the heading 'Why Beer?', E. J. Collier of Cawsand, in East Cornwall, wrote to the press on 27 March 1937: *Sir – Recent interesting letters relating to curious place-names (Hell, Morebath &c.) prompt me to inquire if at any time any ardent advocate of total abstention from alcoholic liquor has ever endeavoured to change the quaint name of the village of Beer (East Devon) to Ginger Pop. Bere is the Anglo-Saxon for barley.*

Within days, the Revd D. R. Blackman of Keyham, Plymouth replied: *Sir – It may be that the inhabitants of Beer know their bible well enough to remember that it means a well of water, and see no need to change a good name (see Numbers xxi, 16), as it provides them with food for thought.*

The interpretation is uncertain, and therefore open to debate. The Saxon version was 'Beerham', or sometimes, 'Berham', whilst in Norman times 'Bera' appeared in the Domesday Book. John Leland, Henry VIII's antiquarian, referred to it as 'Brereworde'. In a petition sent to parliament in 1698, Beer is referred to as 'Beare'. Other variations include Bereword, Bere, and Ber.

Regardless of all this speculation, to my mind, the perfect combination of all things good in life is summed up in the name of a local business: the 'Beer Fish & Chip Shop'!

BEER FISH & CHIP SHOP

Topographically, Beer is one of those places that keeps itself to itself. Whether one rambles eastwards or westwards, it proves to be a shy place that is seen only when almost upon it. If you doubt this notion, stand on Seaton's seafront and look for 'neighbouring' Beer! It cannot be seen. Approach on the coast path from the east, and you will get even closer before you see it. However, the extent of this sheltered settlement is more easily appreciated from the air.

Although a large and long-established village, it's interesting to note that it didn't become a parish in its own right until December 1905.

Many people visit Beer for its shingle beach, which enjoys the great advantage of Beer Head sheltering it from the prevailing south-westerly winds. Those who put to sea often experience different conditions once they have passed beyond this promontory; inexperienced 'sailors' could be lulled into a false sense of security.

It is the sea that has been the livelihood, and sometimes the graveyard, of many a Beer fisherman, or sailor. In August 1859 a snapshot of the fishing industry was provided in a magazine 'cheerfully' named *The Shipwrecked Mariner*:

Beer, just inside the famous "Beer Head", is only a small fishing village, but has several items of interest connected with it... There are about 1,600 inhabitants, of whom about 400 are connected with the sea; and of that number, 100 are fishermen. There is no port or harbour, but being situated in a deep cove, in the bight of the West Bay, there is good anchorage, within shelter of Beer Head. The fishing boats are of two classes: first, – open, deep waisted lug-sail boats, about five tons each; these are employed in trawling, the ground being in the offing, about five miles. The second class are of a similar description, about half the size, and are chiefly employed in shell, herring, and mackerel fishing. The seamen are employed in both foreign and coasting trades; but as there are no ships belonging to Beer, many vessels of other ports are commanded and manned by the seamen of this place; and as navigation is taught in the village, it will account for the proficiency they make when at sea, as they are considered good sailors; and the boatmen are fully equal to the boatmen of Deal.

The number of Beer men serving in the Navy during the French War numbers 167, and

several aged seamen and pensioners are now living here who went through the whole of that war; at the present time, there are a number of men in HM's service; also among the fishermen, a small detachment of "Naval Coastal Volunteers". The trade of the place is chiefly that of fish, which, together with flint, for the potteries, constitutes the sole export; and coals, &c, for the needs of the inhabitants, are the imports... The fishermen have among themselves a friendly society, or club, for relief in sickness and assistance at burial; there are at present about 160 members, and the funds are in a flourishing condition; the whole of their proceedings are marked with the greatest harmony. The female population are employed in the manufacture of the so-called Honiton lace, but which is principally made at Beer, where Her Majesty's nuptial robes were worked.

There is a well worked branch of the Shipwrecked Mariners' Society, under the able superintendence of Lieut. Davies RN, who has about 70 enrolled members, which has been

of great service to the place, having paid for deaths and other casualties of the sea, from 1853 to August 1859, £70.11s.9d, causing in many instances the widow's heart to sing for joy. So much then for Beer with its 1,600 inhabitants, but without a resident clergyman, minister, doctor, or lawyer, and yet crime and disturbance are unknown. The people live to a good old age; sleep and wake without either lock or bolt on their door, or police to protect their property. Should it ever appear that two parties "agree to differ", they do so, and then jump in the same boat together, and all is entirely forgotten.

The full name of the organisation to which he referred was 'The Shipwrecked Fishermen & Mariners' Royal Benevolent Society'.

The Beer fishing boat was a three-masted lugger constructed of elm on an oak frame, built with great skill in the village. The sails were made by Beer fishermen, or their wives. The village had a natural advantage over its local fishing rivals; as already mentioned, Beer Head sheltered it from prevailing winds, which enabled Beer's fishing boats to get out to sea when their neighbours at Branscombe or Seaton were often left on dry land.

This photograph was taken on the beach about a century ago; it portrays almost fifty men and boys. Included within this scene are: sailmaker Ned Marshall (sitting on a crab pot), Jacob Blackmore, Bill Marshall, Tom Russell, Tom Woodgate, Jack Russell, Billy Agland, Jim Bartlett, Billy Rowe, Bobby Driver, Jack Newton, Bill Russell, Theodore Boalch, Dick Ayres, Bill Miller, Albert Ayres, Will Chapple, Ben Potter, Albert Rowe, Billy Woodgate, Bill Orley, George Edwards, Tom White, Bob Gibbs, Jack Ayres, Dan Perry, Frank Thorne, Jim Leyman, Harry Bartlett, William R. Driver, Ern Miller, Norman Miller, Coastguard Triggs, Willie Horner, Jethro Westlake, Joe Russell, Tommy Westlake, Joe Miller. Fred Driver, Thomas and Will Restorick (Thomas is at the back, holding a saw).

Those who appear to be somewhat blurred are guilty of having moved! And only one 'brave' person dared to be captured for all time without some form of head wear.

In the first decade of the twentieth century, Mr Charles G. Harper, a travel writer, made some interesting observations about Beer's fishermen, and the state of the water just offshore:

The fishermen of Beer are a swarthy race, descended, according to tradition, from the crew of a shipwrecked Spanish vessel, who found the place almost depopulated by that plague of which John Starr was a victim. They and their trawlers, which you see laboriously hauled up on the beach, are in the jurisdiction of the port of Exeter.

Here, in the semicircular cove, the summer sea laps softly among the white pebbles, as innocently as though it had never drowned a poor fisherman; and the white of the chalk cliffs, the equal whiteness of the sea-floor and the clearness of the water itself give deep glimpses down to where the seaweed unfurls its banners from rock and cranny, where the crabs are seen walking about, hesitatingly, like octogenarians, and jellyfish float midway, lumps of transparency, like marine ghosts. The sea is green here: a light translucent ghostly green, very beautiful and at the same time, back of one's consciousness − if you examine your feelings − a little mysterious and repellent, suggesting not merely crabs and jellyfish, but inimical unknown things and infinite perils of the deep, sly, malignant, patiently biding their time. The green sea has not the bluff heartiness of the joyous blue.

The little cove, enclosed as it is by cliffs, looks for all the world like a little scene in a little theatre. You almost expect a chorus of fishermen to enter, and hold forth musically on the delights of seine-fishing, but they only suggest to the contemplative stranger that it is "a fine day for a row", and ask, in their rich Devonian tones, if you want a "bwoat",

The white cliffs of Beer are crannied with honeycombings and fissures, banded with black flints, and here and there patterned with ochreous pockets of earth, where the wild flowers grow as though Dame Nature had been making the workaday place gay with bedding plants for the delight of the summer visitors.

Although fishing has been a major industry in the village's economy, whaling hasn't! Many years ago this was written in the local press, and includes the startling revelation that the reporter did not know his fish from his mammals:

A day or two ago an inquiry was made in the columns of the *Gazette* respecting a whale which was seen at Beer. It was stated in reply that the huge fish was towed in by Beer fishermen in 1876, and that very large numbers of persons visited the village for the purpose of seeing the dead monster, which was placed under an awning made of the sails of the fishing fleet. We now give a sketch taken from a photograph of the whale as it lay on the beach. An idea of the girth of the fish will be gathered by comparing it with the man standing by its side.

In order to appreciate the exact size of the unfortunate creature, it would help to know whether the figure in this illustration was either extremely short, or very tall! The whale's jawbone was sent to the Royal Albert Memorial Museum in Exeter.

There have been a few other unusual incidents. In February 1918 a seaplane became stranded on Beer beach, creating much interest amongst the locals. A French ship was torpedoed in March that same year; fifteen mariners were safely landed on Beer's shelving beach.

There was further excitement on 2 September 1938. When fishing off Beer, Fred Newton noticed a great deal of splashing and thrashing about in the water a short distance away. Curiosity

got the better of him, and he went as close as he could get. As luck would have it, he had a camera on board; he managed to take pictures of two enormous creatures, which were a great deal longer than his 25-foot-long fishing boat! They spent a considerable amount of time within 'spitting distance' of Fred's boat. The snaps were developed, and someone suggested that the British Museum of Natural History in London would be able to identify them. Fred had quite a shock when he discovered that these were *Orca gladiator*, more commonly known as the killer whale; the Beer fisherman had possibly come within a whisker of being their next main course! Actually killer whales are members of the

dolphin family, and feed on fishes, squids, sea turtles, and sea birds, but they have been known to attack and mortally wound baleen whales, then leave without eating them, so a tasty little Beer fisherman might well have gone down a treat.

Teenage delinquents are not a modern social problem. There was a time when Beer bred some 'lively' youngsters. This picture shows the demolition of a property on 'Billy Gill's Corner', this being opposite the Dolphin Inn. It was here that some of the village's 'likely lads' gathered. When Florrie Gill lived in the property, she was often the recipient of the attentions of the crowd, which assembled beneath her window at night. They would 'rattle her cage' by tapping on a window. Her response was swift. In those days, when bathrooms were virtually unknown, most folk kept a chamber pot beneath the bed. Florrie's retribution was to open an upstairs window, and anoint the miscreants below.

This meeting place was on a sharp, tight corner. Anyone riding a bicycle down the street, who had to turn right, was obliged to give a clear hand signal. The lads on the corner waited gleefully to firmly shake any outstretched hand as the manoeuvre was completed. Another favourite 'party trick' involved any relatively lightweight Austin Seven that might pass by. As it slowed down to negotiate the bend, some of the stronger Beer lads would lift the back of the vehicle off the ground, literally stopping it in its tracks. Wondering why he wasn't moving, the driver would press hard down on the accelerator. When the engine was fully revved, the lads would lower the vehicle back onto the ground, to watch it shoot off into the distance 'like a bat out of hell'.

It is believed that in the sixteenth century an attempt was made to build a pier, but a storm smashed to pieces the work in progress before it could be of any use.

Beer may not be a harbour, but it still got a passing mention in Boyle and Payne's *Devon Harbours* (1952):

> The true glory of Beer is its fishing boats, and the men who sail them. Vessels from here are famous for their seaworthiness. Although they put out in all weathers – you'll hear it said in neighbouring ports that Beer men are "quite mad" – none are ever lost. Tradition has it that they ride out a storm by making a raft of their smuggled brandy-kegs – almost every Beer man was a smuggler in the days of Jack Rattenbury – which they toss out on their weather beam to break the force of the waves... Be that as it may, they are fine seamen and fine fishermen, their annual catch averaging anything up to 6,000 tons; and Beer itself is an unspoilt and delightful village...

Despite what these authors said, Beer men were not invincible: three fishermen lost their lives in a gale on 3 August 1905 in Beer Roads. More recently, another was lost in the 1980s, and two more in April 1993.

This second extract, from the 1907 publication called *The South Coast of Devon* (C. G. Harper), provides an insight into Beer's most famous son:

> The name of Beer is famous in smuggling annals, for it was in the then rather desperate little fishing village that Jack Rattenbury, smuggler, who lies in Seaton churchyard was born, in 1778. Smugglers and highwaymen in general are figures that loom dimly in the pages of history, and, like figures seen in fog, bulk a good deal larger than they ought. But the famous Jack Rattenbury is an exception. He does not, when we come to close quarters with him, diminish into an undersized, overrated breaker of laws. Instead he grows bigger, the more you learn: and a great deal may be learned of him, for he printed and published the story of his life in 1837.
>
> It seems that he was the son of a Beer shoemaker, who, by going for a sailor and never being heard of again, vindicated the wisdom of that proverb which advises the cobbler to stick to his last. Young Jack Rattenbury never knew his father. He began his adventures at nine years of age, as boy on a fishing-smack, and then became one of the crew of a privateer which set out

from Brixham during the war with France and Spain, to prey upon the enemy: meeting instead, at the very outset, with a French frigate, with the unexpected result that privateer and crew were speedily taken, as prize and prisoners, to Bordeaux. Escaping on an American ship, he at last reached home again, and engaged for a time in fishing. But fishing was poor employment for an adventurous spirit, and Rattenbury soon found his way into smuggling. He first took part in the exploits of a Lyme Regis boat, trading in that illegitimate way to the Channel Islands, and then found more lawful employment on a brig called *The Friends of Beer and Seaton*. But the very first trip was disastrous. Sailing from Bridport to Tenby, for culm, he again experienced capture: by a French privateer on this occasion. The privateer put out a prize-crew of four men on the brig, with orders to take her to the nearest French port. "Then," says Rattenbury, "when the privateer was gone, the prize-master ordered me to go

aloft and loose the main-topgallant sail. When I came down, I perceived that he was steering very wildly, through ignorance of the coast, and I offered to take the helm, to which he consented, and directed me to steer south-east by north. He then went below, and was engaged in drinking and carousing with his companions. They likewise sent me up a glass of grog occasionally, which animated my spirits, and I began to conceive a hope, not only of escaping, but also of being revenged on the enemy." The artful Rattenbury then steered up to Portland, and when the master asked what land it was, replied "Alderney". Presently they came off St Aldhelm's Head, and were distinctly suspicious when told it was Cape La Hogue.

"We were now within a league of Swanage, and I persuaded them to go on shore to get a pilot. They then hoisted out a boat, into which I got with three of them. We now came so close to shore that people hailed us. My companions began to swear, and said the people spoke English. This I denied, and urged them to hail again; but as they were rising to do so, I plunged overboard, and came up on the other side of the boat. They then struck at me with their oars, and snapped a pistol at me, but it missed fire. The boat in which they were now took water, and finding they were engaged in a vain pursuit that the *Nancy*, revenue cutter, went in pursuit of the brig and, recapturing her, brought her into Cowes the same night."

He was then forcibly enlisted in the Navy by the Press Gang, and, escaping from His Majesty's service, went cod-fishing off Newfoundland. Returning, the ship he was on was captured by a Spanish privateer and taken into Vigo. Escaping with his usual dexterity, he reached home and added another thrilling item to his hazardous career by getting married, April 17th, 1801. After a quiet interval of piloting, he resumed smuggling, in earnest; with the usual ups and downs of fortune incidental to that shy trade.

Having made several successful voyages, and feeling pretty confident, he went ashore to carouse with some friends in one of the old taverns of Beer. In the same room were a sergeant and several privates of the South Devon Militia, among others. "After drinking two or three pots of beer," he says, "the sergeant, whose name was Hill, having heard my name mentioned by some of my companions, went out with his men, and soon they returned again, having armed themselves with swords and muskets. The sergeant then advanced towards me and said, 'You are my prisoner. You are a deserter, and must go along with me.' For a moment I was much terrified, knowing that if was taken I should, in all probability go aboard in the fleet; and this wrought up my mind to a pitch of desperation. I endeavoured, however, to keep as cool as possible, and in answer to his charge, I said, 'Sergeant, you are surely labouring under an error; I have done nothing that can authorise you in taking me up or detaining me. You must certainly have mistaken me for some other person'."

View from Smuggler's Cave, Beer.

This shows us, pretty clearly, that someone must have written Rattenbury's reminiscences for him. He probably was incapable of such book-English, and certainly would not have spoken anything else than the broadest of Devonshire speech. However, he describes how he drew the sergeant into a parley and how, while it was going on, he jumped through a trap-door into the cellar. "I then threw off my jacket and shirt, to prevent any one from holding me, and having armed myself with a reaping-hook and a knife, which I had in my pocket, I threw myself into an attitude of defence at the entrance, which was a half-hatch door, the lower part of which I shut, and then declared that I would kill the first man who came near me, and that I would not be taken from the spot alive. At this the sergeant was terrified; but he said to his men, 'Soldiers do your duty; advance and seize him.' To which they replied 'Sergeant, you proposed it; take the lead and set us an example, and we will follow.' No one offered to advance, and I remained in the position I have described for four hours, holding them at bay."

The sergeant sent for aid, but before that arrived the women of Beer rushed in with an artful story of shipwreck, attracting the soldiers' attention. Rattenbury, seizing the opportunity,

dashed among them, half-naked, and escaped to the beach, where he hastily took boat and went off to his own vessel, and safety.

In 1806 he, his crew, and his cargo of spirit-tubs were captured by the *Duke of York* cutter, when returning from Alderney. He was fined £100, and with his companions was sentenced to the alternative imprisonment or service on board a man-o'-war. They chose the sea, and were accordingly shipped on board the brig *Kate*, in the Downs; but soon, while the officers were all more or less drunk, he found an opportunity of escaping, and was presently home again.

The smuggling exploits of this master of the art were endless. Perhaps the most amusing – to the reader, at any rate – is that incident at Seaton Hole, where, one dark night, going up the cliff with a keg on his back, one of a cargo he had just landed, he was so unfortunate as to stumble over a donkey, which began to bray so horribly that, with his trumpeting and the noise of the smuggler's fall, a Revenue officer, sleeping at the post of duty, was aroused, and seized forty kegs, nearly the whole of that run.

After serving three terms of imprisonment for smuggling, and for being unable to pay a fine of £4,500, Rattenbury's many adventures came to an end in 1833. His later years were devoted to fishing and piloting, and between whiles, to composing his reminiscences. In those pages you read this rather pitiful note: "The smuggler gratefully acknowledges the kindness of the Right Honourable Lord Rolle, who now allows him one shilling per week for life." What lavish generosity!

That was a picturesque village in which this Old Master and prime exponent of smuggling lived. The one street led steeply down to the sea, with a clear rivulet purling along the gutter, with quaint pumps at intervals and bordered by cob cottages. The peasant women sat at the doors making the pillow lace of Devonshire, and the children, for lack of better toys, played the great game of "shop" with the fish-offal in the kennel.

A Street in Beer

But the old Beer of this picture has vanished, and a new and smart village has arisen in its stead, with just two or three of these characteristic survivals, to make us bitterly regret that which we have lost ...

Nicknamed 'The Rob Roy of the West', he survived many run-ins with the authorities, until his adventures were severely curtailed by a bad bout of gout. Ultimately he achieved a level of respectability; he retired to Sidmouth and wrote M*emoirs of a Smuggler*, which was published in 1837. Today Rattenbury Cottages are named after this much-vaunted villain!

The numerous kegs of craftily smuggled brandy were circulated throughout East Devon. An expression in the district implicated other villages in the illegal trade: "Sidbury financed – Branscombe landed – Sidmouth found wages, and Salcombe (Regis) carriers." Jack Rattenbury was aided by associates throughout East Devon; most of them firmly believed that what they were doing was not morally wrong, just outside the law and tax system of the country.

Whether all the stories of derring-do attributed to him are true, we shall never know: time has probably enhanced his reputation. However, in recent years the village has staged 'Rattenbury Day', when it's possible for visitors to buy a 'passport' to the village of 'Free Beer'. On such occasions the village celebrates with exhibitions, demonstrations, displays, activities, entertainments, boat rides, lugger racing and so on to raise money for local and national charities.

Most people think of Devon as a county of red cliffs, but those who bask in the sun at Beer are almost dazzled by the white rock exposures. *Black's Guide to Devon* (1871) acknowledged the striking coastal scenery of the district:

A small stream trickles through a narrow defile into the sea at Beer, a mere scattering of fishermen's cottages upon a romantic beach. The lofty cliffs now stretch away westward like the huge rampart of some Titanic stronghold; flushing into a myriad different hues when the sunlight falls upon them…

CASTLE ROCKS & BRANSCOMBE BEACH

The coast path, southwards to Beer Head and then westwards over Beer Common towards Branscombe, makes a fine walk with terrific views. A description is included in another of my books, *Walk the East Devon Coast – Lyme Regis to Lympstone*.

Just to the west of Beer Head, the Under Hooken Landslip is one of a number of examples of subsidence on a grand scale, impressive evidence of an unstable cliff-line. Before 1788 the cliffs rose almost vertically from the sea, which lapped at their base hundreds of feet below. However, an underground stream percolating through these rocks, which emerged about half way down (or up!) the cliff, became obstructed and its subterranean waters were ponded back. Not being able to escape, they spread out underground over the marls lying within the cliff; in doing so, they lubricated the surface of these rocks. In the late eighteenth century a great fissure appeared on top of the cliffs, and some ten acres of land were cut off. This isolated feature was to stay in place until

one night in March 1790, when the whole of it slipped some 250 feet. This created a ridge in the seabed extending a few hundred yards beyond the normal shoreline. The consequences were spectacular. Crab pots laid down in the water, just the night before, were marooned more than 15 feet above the surface! Since then nature has taken over. A succession of plants, shrubs, bushes and trees have colonised this landslip and draped it in greenery to produce an amazing habitat. It's possible to walk down through this mini-Devonshire jungle; although not as spectacular, or as extensive, as the Dowlands and other landslips between Seaton and Lyme, it is, nevertheless, worth the effort.

If you walk the coastline with a detailed map, you will notice Sherborne Rocks marked on it. Before the Norman Conquest the manor belonged to the Abbey of Horton, but was annexed in 1122 (with all its possessions) to the Abbey of Sherborne. The sheltered south-facing slopes above Beer's first vicarage (see map on page 16) were once the vineyards where the abbots grew their grapes for making wine. The question is, would they have had the marketing wit, or nerve, to label it 'Beer Wine' in order to confuse tipplers? Many years after the domestic growing of grapes had finished, local people would forage for, and still find, wild grapes.

Long before the days of sophisticated methods of weather forecasting, the people of Beer had their own, almost foolproof, way of discovering whether it would be a dry summer, or a wet one. A hundred-year-old white elm tree had a remarkable habit each spring of blooming with either white leaves, thus assuring locals of a fine dry summer, or with green leaves to forewarn of a damp and dreary one. Unfortunately this meteorological marvel, at Townsend in Beer, became dangerous and had to be felled.

Running along the village's main street is the Brook, a feature in which all Beer boys had to fall, at least once, before they were regarded as Beer men.

This water supply has a history, and many people visiting the village are curious about the conduits. Their story was told in the press in 1859:

As the subject of Drinking Fountains is at the present time engaging considerable attention, a description of those at Beer may be acceptable. To persons unacquainted with the locality it may be briefly stated that Beer is... one of the bye-nooks of England which has scarcely altered in its external characteristics in more than two hundred years, and is much admired by artists for its picturesque beauties. The inhabitants are noted for longevity, and there is a general absence of epidemic diseases, which may, in a great measure, be attributed to the abundant supply of the purest water, added to the mild climate of the sheltered valley in which Beer is situated. In the upper part of the valley three springs unite to form a small rivulet or

brook, which comes down through the place. In very ancient times it turned a mill, of which some remains may still exist. Then, until the year 1835, the brook took pretty much its own course. In 1835 it was confined in a stone channel, at an expense of £70, by public subscription of the inhabitants. Though still called the "brook", it now performs the part of a rapid and fairly respectable gutter, running at the rate of six miles per hour, which, carrying off into the sea all impurities, is, no doubt, of the highest sanitary benefit. It is one of the streams…to turn to… for a supply of drinking water. This spring (the third and lowermost) issues at the foot of a low hill of limestone formation, and is received into a covered reservoir of 12 feet square and four feet deep, built of freestone over the spring, and further protected by a covering of tenacious clay. It therefore rises into something like an ice-house, enjoying perfect coolness and

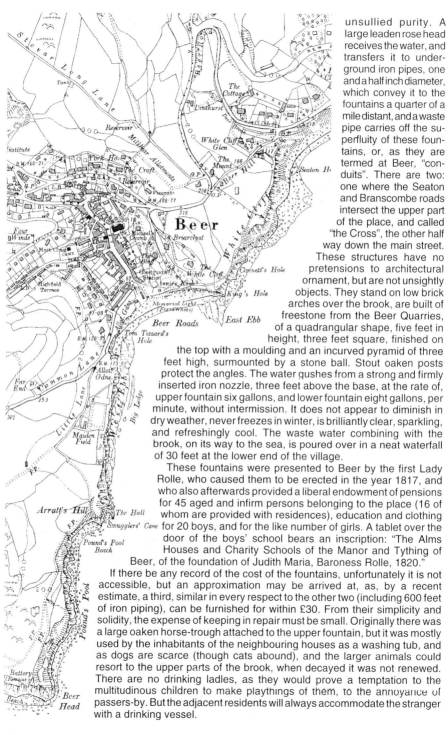

unsullied purity. A large leaden rose head receives the water, and transfers it to underground iron pipes, one and a half inch diameter, which convey it to the fountains a quarter of a mile distant, and a waste pipe carries off the superfluity of these fountains, or, as they are termed at Beer, "conduits". There are two: one where the Seaton and Branscombe roads intersect the upper part of the place, and called "the Cross", the other half way down the main street. These structures have no pretensions to architectural ornament, but are not unsightly objects. They stand on low brick arches over the brook, are built of freestone from the Beer Quarries, of a quadrangular shape, five feet in height, three feet square, finished on the top with a moulding and an incurved pyramid of three feet high, surmounted by a stone ball. Stout oaken posts protect the angles. The water gushes from a strong and firmly inserted iron nozzle, three feet above the base, at the rate of, upper fountain six gallons, and lower fountain eight gallons, per minute, without intermission. It does not appear to diminish in dry weather, never freezes in winter, is brilliantly clear, sparkling, and refreshingly cool. The waste water combining with the brook, on its way to the sea, is poured over in a neat waterfall of 30 feet at the lower end of the village.

These fountains were presented to Beer by the first Lady Rolle, who caused them to be erected in the year 1817, and who also afterwards provided a liberal endowment of pensions for 45 aged and infirm persons belonging to the place (16 of whom are provided with residences), education and clothing for 20 boys, and for the like number of girls. A tablet over the door of the boys' school bears an inscription: "The Alms Houses and Charity Schools of the Manor and Tything of Beer, of the foundation of Judith Maria, Baroness Rolle, 1820."

If there be any record of the cost of the fountains, unfortunately it is not accessible, but an approximation may be arrived at, as, by a recent estimate, a third, similar in every respect to the other two (including 600 feet of iron piping), can be furnished for within £30. From their simplicity and solidity, the expense of keeping in repair must be small. Originally there was a large oaken horse-trough attached to the upper fountain, but it was mostly used by the inhabitants of the neighbouring houses as a washing tub, and as dogs are scarce (though cats abound), and the larger animals could resort to the upper parts of the brook, when decayed it was not renewed. There are no drinking ladles, as they would prove a temptation to the multitudinous children to make playthings of them, to the annoyance of passers-by. But the adjacent residents will always accommodate the stranger with a drinking vessel.

The event of the erection was commemorated by a poetical attempt from an aged woman of Beer, in humble life. It is rather lengthy, and as the feeling expressed is better than the execution, the concluding stanzas only are given –

And whilst you view the streams each day,
For your kind benefactress pray
That still her life may be prolonged,
With health and every blessing crowned.
For, doubtless, till the end of time
The conduits ever shall remain
To show to all, both far and near,
What Lady Rolle has done for Beer.

Both the patroness and the poetess have long since departed to their rest.

Beer Village, near Seaton, Devon

Apart from the two stone conduits, lower down the main street, by what is now 'the Gallery', there was also a cast-iron fountain. Nearby are Fountain Cottages.

In 1989 the brook was the centre of a controversy after a prolonged spell of dry weather. The stream has never been known to dry up and villagers became extremely annoyed as they watched a thousand gallons of water per hour tumbling past, knowing that they were not allowed to extract much-needed water for their parched gardens and shrivelled-up flower beds. In a year, the total permitted to be taken out was the same as one hour's flow. The ridiculous element is that it pours into the sea at the bottom of the village, and is lost forever, doing nobody any good!

The village's main street has been severely flooded on at least two occasions. In July 1926 a ferocious summer storm resulted in torrents of water pouring down from the steep hills above the village. This happened so quickly that the ground could not absorb the water; at the low point of the village centre, shops and houses were swamped. This particular picture was of another major inundation in the early 1960s.

The following appeared in the local press, on 1 November 1900, revealing the immense skill and enterprise of some local ladies:

An interesting account of the lace industry carried on at Beer and Branscombe is in the current number of *The Lady*. The villages are spoken of as two "of the prettiest and most delightful" in Devonshire. Their beauties have, indeed, attracted the eye of many an artist, including Mr John White RI. But the great interest of Beer lies in the fact that some of the best Honiton lace has been made there ever since the early part of the 19th century. The Queen's lace wedding gown was made by Beer women. Miss Jane Bidney secured the order, and she resided in Beer while the gown was being made. The design of the wedding gown consisted of flowers and leaves whose initials spelt the name of "Adelaide", in compliment to the Queen of William IV, who was a very affectionate aunt to the young Princess Victoria. The gown cost £1,000.

Having thus won their laurels the Beer lace makers found a great demand for their work. The tide of fashion set in their direction for a few years, but gradually decreased. The industry, however, was revived under the care of Miss Constance Blenet and Miss Bowden, who taught the women how to make the beautiful Italian and Flemish laces. A little later on... Miss Trevelyan took the work up, and at the Chicago Exhibition was awarded a medal for the copies of Italian laces. Since then she has taken care that the Beer and Branscombe workers have been well represented at exhibitions, and has got them a great deal of work on commission; but she insists on the very best lace, and keeps about 12 women employed in the former and eight women employed in the latter village. Still, she says, there is work for many more if they would undertake it. She sent some lovely lace to the Paris Exhibition, with the real old "vrai beseau" ground, and obtained a bronze and also a silver medal. Mrs Fowler also had an award.

Queen Victoria's wedding dress was trimmed with lace, which took more than a hundred lace-workers longer than six months to make: from May to November 1839. The final cost was £1,000 – enough to have bought several cottages in Beer at that time. Afterwards the designs were destroyed to ensure that they could not be copied. The Queen must have been delighted with the quality of the work, because she later ordered a black shawl from Beer.

Like many villagers, Miss Bidney had never left the county before; to her, London was a world away. Apparently, while she was waiting to be received by Queen Victoria, she was so nervous that she fainted. Having regained her composure, she was commanded to attend the wedding. In 1982 the wedding flounce was brought back to Beer to be exhibited in St Michael's Church, as part of the Axe Valley Maritime Exhibition.

The picture shows a pillow lace worker concentrating on the task in hand. Locally there are some who still make pillow, bone or Devon lace.

As an enthusiast of all things about Devon, I have been invited to give talks in a considerable number of public halls around Devon. Some are quite stark, while others are more homely and welcoming. The Mariners' Hall, built on the site of some demolished cottages close to the parish church, clearly falls into the latter category. Opened in September 1958, it was a gift to the village from Mr Arthur Edward Good, a mariner himself. The building was designed by Mr F. S. Kett, an Axminster architect who decided on a grey exterior to complement the neighbouring parish church.

The initial management committee chairman was Mr D. O. Good, who received the deeds from his uncle. At the opening ceremony, Mr A. E. Good told the audience that it had always been his desire to commemorate those sons of Beer who had gone forth from the village to follow the true tradition of the sea. At this moving ceremony, Beer's then oldest retired mariner, 85-year-old Joe Bartlett, presented Mrs Good with a bouquet.

In 1969 an enhancement scheme brought the hall up to an even higher standard of accommodation, making it one of the best in the county.

This is our third and final contribution from the forthright Mr Charles G. Harper. As you see, he wasn't compelled to sweet-talk about the places he described. This is what he said in 1907:

There was once a humble little church in this same street of Beer. A very humble church, but in keeping with the place. And now? Why a large and highly ornate building, infinitely pretentious and big enough for a cathedral, has arisen on the site of it… There are polished marbles in this new church of Beer, where there should be rough-axed masonry, and a suburban high finish in place of rustic rudeness; and the sole relics of what had once been are the two memorial tablets, themselves sufficiently rural. One is to "John, the fifth son of William Starr of Bere, Gent., and Dorothy his

wife, which died in the plague was here buried 1646." John Starr was one of a family which, about a century earlier, had become owners of a moiety of the manor. The house he built in

Beer's street bears on one chimney the initials "J S" and on another a star, in punning allusion to his name.

The other memorial in the church is to "Edward Good, late and industrious fisherman, who left to the Vicar and Churchwardens for the time being and their successors for ever twenty pounds in trust for the Poor of this Parish. The interest to be distributed at Christmas in the proportion of two thirds at Beer and one at Seaton. He died November 7, 1804, in the sixty seventh year of his age."

Beer's church of St Michael's is on the eastern, or left, side of the main street leading down to the sea. Dating back to 1878, it is a beautiful building.

This is how the press reported the laying of the foundation stone ceremony, a year earlier, in 1877:

Great interest was excited in the picturesque village of Beer, near Seaton, on Thursday last, when the cornerstone of the church, now being built, was laid by the Hon. Mark Rolle. The form of prayer adopted was the one sanctioned by several of the Bishops, and was read by the vicar (the Revd H. Vyvyan). After the hymn had been sung the stone which rested on the wall was raised, and a record of the event, written on vellum and attested by the signatures of the vicar, the churchwardens (messrs Evans and Hammett), and the architects, was placed in a glass-stoppered bottle, and deposited in a recess made in the stone beneath, and covered with a piece of slate secured with cement. Mr Rolle then, with a silver trowel, proceeded to lay the bed of mortar under the stone, which was then lowered, and, after striking it thrice said: "In the faith of Jesus Christ, we place this cornerstone in the name of God the Father, God the Son, and God the Holy Ghost. Amen." The short service being ended, Mr Rolle briefly addressed the large number of persons present. Holding up the trowel, he first expressed his gratification at the kindness of the inhabitants of Beer in presenting him with the handsome implement he had just used, which he should always greatly value. He then said how rejoiced he was at the work having been thus happily commenced, and expressed a hope that in the summer of next year they would all meet again and witness the consecration of a building which prayer would be constantly heard, and spiritual comfort given to future generations. The number of persons present was very large, and all were very glad to see that Mr Rolle was accompanied by Lady Gertrude and their daughter. In the evening the workmen had a substantial supper, supplied by Mrs Good, at the Dolphin Inn, and presided over by Mr Harris, the Clerk of the Works, Mr Hampton, the foreman, acting as vice-president. The old church, or chapel, as it was more properly called, was originally a small structure, built in the decorated style, but was subsequently greatly enlarged, and filled with heavy galleries, and having become greatly dilapidated, Mr Rolle generously determined to erect a large and handsome church in place of it. Consulting the comfort and convenience of the inhabitants, he decided to build it on the same site, in the centre of the village. The church will accommodate 500 adults and 130 children. It will have a lofty nave, with clerestory, north and south aisles, chancel, transepts, and a tower capped with a square spire at the north-west angle of the building. The floor of the nave will be $3\frac{1}{2}$ feet above the level of that of the old church, and the floor of the church will be 3 feet higher. This is necessary from the great rise of the ground on which the new church is being built. Some extra expense will thus be caused, but the architectural effect of the building will be enhanced. The church has been designed by messrs Hayward and Sons of Exeter, messrs Stephens and Bastow, of Bristol, are the builders, and Mr Harris is Clerk of the Works. The handsome silver trowel, with its oak handle, made from a piece of the timber of the old church, was supplied by messrs Ellis, of Exeter. The estimated cost of the new church is £6,000.

The church was duly consecrated on 9 August 1878.

The Right Revd the Lord Bishop of Exeter on Friday consecrated the new Church of St Michael's ... The old church or chapel of St Michael had been for many years in a dilapidated state, and was inadequate for the wants of the parishioners. The original structure, so far as could be ascertained by the remains of the chancel arch and east window, was erected in the very beginning of the 14th century, and was of small extent, the width not exceeding 12 feet. Additions were made from time to time to increase the accommodation, until the width of the church became greater than the length, and the interior was filled with narrow high pews and heavy galleries. It was under these circumstances that the Hon Mark Rolle determined to build a new church, and early in 1874 he called in the services of Mr Hayward of Exeter, to make a survey and report as to the most suitable site for it. Three sites were thought to be eligible, and after mature deliberation Mr Rolle decided to have the church built on that of the old structure, on the ground that it would best meet the conveniences of the feelings of

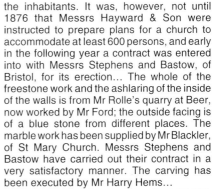

the inhabitants. It was, however, not until 1876 that Messrs Hayward & Son were instructed to prepare plans for a church to accommodate at least 600 persons, and early in the following year a contract was entered into with Messrs Stephens and Bastow, of Bristol, for its erection... The whole of the freestone work and the ashlaring of the inside of the walls is from Mr Rolle's quarry at Beer, now worked by Mr Ford; the outside facing is of a blue stone from different places. The marble work has been supplied by Mr Blackler, of St Mary Church. Messrs Stephens and Bastow have carried out their contract in a very satisfactory manner. The carving has been executed by Mr Harry Hems...

The cost of the church will be about £7,000. We understand that at no very distant time the east and west windows are to be filled with stained glass.

There were great celebrations in the village: floral arches were constructed in the main street, bands played, and the fishermen organised a procession that included a lugger, which was lifted up onto wheels and sailed up the main street with all its sails set!

Old picture postcards show the church with a spire atop its tower, but today it's gone. It suffered several blows in its relatively short life. A mine, which went off in the sea just a short distance offshore, shook it up, and a lightning strike rendered it so unsafe that it had to be taken down in 1962. Steeplejacks from Nottingham were entrusted with the difficult task of dismantling it; some of the larger blocks had to be cut down before they could be removed.

The Congregational church is blessed with a Wurlitzer organ. It claims to be the first instrument of its kind to be installed in this country.

In 1821 Lord Rolle paid for the building of a row of ten almshouses in the village. Two schoolrooms were added each end at a later date, one for the boys, the other for the girls. A Devonshire Directory states that: *The late Lady Rolle left £3,900 consols to found almshouses here for 25 poor men and 20 women, and also £3,100 of the same stock to clothe and educate 20 boys and 20 girls.*

In honour of his late wife, the schools were known as the "Charity Schools of the Manor and Tything of Beer of the Foundation of Judith Maria Baroness Rolle". I would imagine that in daily conversation most Beer folk would have shortened the title!

The schools were reorganised in the 1870s. Further change occurred when the Board of Education was formed in 1899. The management of voluntary schools was passed over to local education authorities. When Mark Rolle, Lord of the Manor, died in 1907, his successor Lord Clinton did not wish to continue the family patronage of the schools, so an historic link was severed. In 1914 Mr Rendel Page was in charge of the Public Elementary School whilst Miss Elizabeth Pike was mistress at the Infants' School.

Between 1929 and 1931, the mixed school building was rebuilt and enlarged, and the schools were combined into a Church of England Elementary School. This was officially opened by the Bishop of Exeter on 16 April 1931.

But nothing in education remains the same for long. In 1948 senior pupils over the age of eleven years, who to date could have spent their entire educational life in the village, were obliged to continue their educations at Colyton or Axminster: which one depended largely on their ability, the former being a Grammar School, the latter a Secondary Modern School.

In September 1979, the junior school moved to new purpose-built premises high up the hill in Mare Lane, where it remains to this day. The sounds of happy children at play can be heard over the rooftops of properties lying below the school.

Passing mention has already been made about Beer and its attraction to artists.

One of these past masters of the canvas merits a special mention. Here is the report of the unveiling of his memorial in March 1897:

A distinguished gathering of artists and others took place at the quaint village of Beer on the occasion of the unveiling of a memorial to the late Mr Hamilton Macallum, an eminent painter, who at times resided at Beer, and whose talents were largely devoted to representing the charming scenery of the neighbourhood. The weather was delightfully fine, and the

proceedings took place under the most favourable auspices. The memorial is situated on the sea cliff at the bottom end of the main street of the village. That side of it which faces the sea consists of a medallion in bronze relief, giving a faithful likeness to the late artist embedded in a large square block of Portland stone. Underneath is the inscription 'Hamilton Macallum, Born 22nd March, 1841; Died 23rd June, 1896'… Wreaths were placed upon the memorial and there was also a garland of flowers from the fisher boys.

There are seats either side. On the reverse of the memorial was an aneroid barometer, which was presented by Mr R. Holman.

Another account of the proceedings added these details:

Saturday was an eventful day in the history of the picturesque and romantic fishing village of Beer, which nestles so peacefully between and beneath the high cliffs mid-way between Sidmouth and Seaton. It has always been a favourite resort of artists, but no one loved it more than the late Mr Hamilton Macallum, who made it his chief resort for nearly thirty years, and not only revelled in the beauties of the neighbourhood, but took an active interest in the well-being of the inhabitants. If it did much to help the artist on to fame, he did a great deal to enhance its renown. There he most loved to linger quietly in the bright sunshine, and it was there that he passed peacefully away last year in the sunny month of June. When his many friends and brother artists decided to erect some memorial to his memory they felt that no more appropriate site could be selected than the scene of his labours; and the movement was freely entered into by the inhabitants, a committee being formed with Mr George Gibbons as Chairman, Mr J. Perkins, hon sec, and Mr R. Skinner as hon treasurer, whilst Mr John White RI, and Mr J. Hodgson Liddell represented art. The Hon Mark Rolle gave the matter his support, and at once dedicated a piece of waste land facing the cove as a public resort, and at his own expense it has been prettily laid out and fenced in, under the direction of Mr Hayman, sub-agent…

Mr George Gibson opened the proceedings by asking Professor Herkomer to unveil the memorial, which could not be a more appropriate site as it was in front of the scene Mr Macallum so dearly loved to paint, and also the beach where he spent so many hours, and in

front of the house where he passed so peacefully away… Mr E. Chamier accepted the charge of the memorial on behalf of the Hon Mark Rolle, Mr George Gibbons, Mr R. Skinner, and Mr J. Hodgson Liddell, trustees appointed. Mr Macallum was so well-known and respected in Beer, however that he was sure that every man, woman, and child in the village would be a trustee of the monument. Mr Chamier also declared the grounds forever open to the public, to be maintained by the Hon Mark Rolle. (Applause.) Mr MacWhirter RA, said: It's right and appropriate that a memorial to Hamilton Macallum should face out to the sea. He loved the sea from his very youth. Born in the far north, where the sea is greyer and wilder, he began by painting those. He painted the seas in the far south of sunny Italy, but he always came back to these shores. It is right and proper that the fishermen he loved should see this monument as they go out to their work, and also when they return from it in the evening. It is fortunate, and also appropriate, that the sunshine upon us today, and upon this memorial to our friend, for he himself was a sunny man, and of a breezy temperament, and loved to paint the sunshine rather than the storm. You have here something more than a monument; you have in your town here a work of art, and you might have gone to the ends of the earth before you would have found a more loving friend than Mr E. Onslow Ford, or a more distinguished sculptor. I ask you to give him a vote of thanks for his handsome and artistic memorial. (Applause) Mr E. Onslow Ford RA said: I thank you for the hearty manner in which you have appreciated this effort. Mr Macallum was one of the first artists whose

acquaintance I made when I came to London, and his works were always a delight to me. It was a great pleasure for me to be associated with his older friends in erecting this memorial.

The proceedings then terminated.

A number of important people attended this touching ceremony, including Frederick J. Widgery, another well-known Devonshire artist, whose father erected a cross on Brat Tor, on Dartmoor, to commemorate Queen Victoria's Golden Jubilee. Both Widgerys were fine landscape artists, and F. J., who was Mayor of Exeter three times, was honoured by the city when it came to choosing car registration letters. Exeter-registered cars carried the letters 'FJ' until the new system of registration for cars was commenced in 2001.

In 1897, when Queen Victoria's Diamond Jubilee was celebrated in Beer, the gardens on the slopes above the beach were laid out in her honour, and accordingly named 'The Jubilee Gardens'.

Beer is not the sort of place in which people find themselves by accident. Those who reach the village usually do so by choice. The nature of the topography means that the roads which lead down into it are generally fairly steep. It also means that there was never any chance that Beer could be linked to a railway. In the days when Seaton had its own branch line terminus, Beer had a bus depot; the bus ferried passengers to and from the railway.

Lying to the west of the village, 'Beer Quarry Caves' are unique. The best way to learn about them is to make a visit, but take a pullover, as it's always about 11 degrees Celsius in the caves regardless of the temperature outside! They are open during the summer season, and excellent guided one-hour tours provide people with an unforgettable experience.

This was written in 1887:

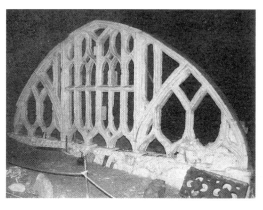

In medieval times the churches and mansions of Devon were built to a large extent of Beer stone, and the same material was used for the construction of great buildings in other parts of the kingdom. Mr P. E. Massey, an architect... says that the ancient crypt Chapel of St Stephen's, Westminster, is built of it; and that he has in his possession a pinnacle of William of Wykeham's work in Winchester Cathedral, of 14th century date, well preserved, though it has been exposed over the north aisle for nearly 500 years. He cites, also, as proofs of its durability, its uses in churches of the county, built from the 11th to the 16th centuries, and declares that on examining these edifices he has found the condition of the stone generally to be good, instances of decay being invariably attributable to the builders having failed to set the stone in its natural bed. At Axminster, Axmouth, and Lyme Regis, Norman work in Beer stone may still be seen, and the fine old Norman doorway at the first-named place is proudly mentioned as proof of the power of the material to resist the destructive influence of ages. Of the same stone the window-mullions of the neglected church of St Pancras, Exeter, is composed, and they have stood the test of 600 years. Portions of Exeter Cathedral are of Beer stone. The beautifully-decorated Oldham and Speke chapels in that grand old fane are formed of it. As a further proof of its excellence, we may mention that Beer stone was chosen for the two most exquisite examples of ecclesiastical-stonework in all England – the sedilia of Exeter Cathedral, and Bishop Percy's chapel at Beverley. Modern examples of its adaptability are to be found in the churches of Eastbourne and Beer, the Roman Catholic churches at Portsmouth and Brighton, the Baptist chapels at Hereford and Ross, and the mansion now in course of erection for Sir Henry Peek at Rousdon.

BEER QUARRIES 1300B

Soon after the Great Western Railway rendered the quarries of Bath stone accessible, the demand for Beer stone fell off, and the Bath came into favour. It's admitted, too, that the production of the Beer Quarries fell into disrepute from quantities of material overlaying the good stratum, and mixed with flint, having been sent into the market. The construction, a few years back, of a junction railway to Seaton, within 2 or 3 miles of Beer,

enabled the lessees of the Quarries to compete once more with the Bath stone. With a view of working the old Quarries spiritedly, the Beer Freestone and Lime Company (Limited) was formed about twelve months since, and arrangements have now been made for supplying the stone at a reasonable cost to builders in all parts of the country. The stone is composed of carbonate of lime, silica, and grit. Special merit is claimed for it by account of possessing a larger percentage of silica than other stones, so that while it's as easy as Bath stone to work, by exposure it becomes as hard as Portland stone...

In addition to the many thousands of visitors of the general public, the caves have also been visited by all sorts of groups down the years. One of these groups came in late July 1937. The *Devon & Exeter Gazette* were on hand to report the experience:

Despite unfavourable weather, there was a large attendance of members of the Devon Archaeological Exploration Society at Beer on Saturday, when a visit was paid to the famous

Beer Quarries and to prehistoric excavations in Conehill Valley between Seaton and Beer. At the quarries the guide to the party was the foreman (Mr P. Franklin), who has worked at the quarries for 23 years, his father (Mr Henry Franklin), having been employed there for half a century. With torches and candles, the party listened to Mr Franklin, 90 feet below the surface, explain the history of the quarries, and how the quarries hewed out in blocks which averaged between 3 and 4 tons. The visitors then crossed the road to the old quarry, where they saw the Roman and Norman underground workings. Experts thought – said the guide – that bronzed tools were used in carrying out the work. Up to 1885 the men of Beer used picks and blasting material. The durability of the Beer stone was evidenced at many of the churches in Devon and other counties... The visitors were greatly impressed by the Norman work traced in the arches and roof and with the cave where smugglers in the olden days hid tea, coffee, and rum, which they afterwards took to Honiton to sell, returned to Beer to work with their colleagues in the quarry. It is believed that the renowned smuggler, Jack Rattenbury, was the leader, that he had several caves along the Devonshire coast.

Occasionally special events have been staged at the quarries. This exciting one, in August 1931, showed off the skills of a local rescue group:

The Roman and Norman quarries… the only underground quarries in Devon, were illuminated with hundreds of candles on Saturday and presented a fairyland spectacle, especially the so-called Norman chapel and the Smugglers' Cave. There are no stalactites at Beer, but the excavations are natural, and on the south side must have been done many hundreds of years ago, as Exeter Cathedral and most of the West Country churches have Beer stone more or less in them, as was remarked by the Bishop of Exeter a week ago. On Saturday there was the added attraction of a demonstration at the quarries by the Beer Rocket Apparatus Company and His Majesty's Coastguards, under the direction of Captain Betts, Inspector of the Southern Division of Coastguards. An interesting display was witnessed by over one thousand residents and visitors. First a rocket was fired from the plateau adjoining the disused lime kilns carrying a light line, followed by larger ropes carrying the breeches buoy to a pole on the Roman side of the quarries. A Boy Scout was then brought safely "ashore" amidst the cheers of the spectators, and afterwards was "restored" as if from drowning. Captain Betts gave a running description of the work of rescue and restoration in a lucid and sometimes humorous vein. He strongly advised all present, in case of emergency, never to give those suffering from any kind of accident causing unconsciousness any form of alcohol, as it would be likely to cause choking. People generally rushed for brandy, or even whisky, but if it was brought it would probably be drunk by the men doing the rescue work and do them more good. (Laughter.)… At the close Mr E. Terrell, Managing Director of the Beer Stone Company, who gave the site for quarterly practices, and annual display, proposed, on behalf of the Company and the visitors, a hearty vote of thanks to Captain Betts and the Coastguards and the Rocket Company, the latter composed of Beer fishermen. This was carried by cheers.

Medals were presented amid cheers to three of the Beer men who had put in 20 years service with the Lifesaving Rocket Company – Messrs Richard Westlake, William White, and William John Woodgate. Several of those present had previously qualified.

One of Beer's more unusual, but important, industries of the past was the manufacture of gun flints. Dark flints embedded in the chalk cliffs were extracted for this purpose.

It is thought that Beer supplied over half of the raw materials for the flintlocks used by the Parliamentarian forces during the English Civil War (1642–1646). Many years later, a local manufacturer, who had won contracts with both the army and the navy, supplied large numbers of gun flints. The trade died when some bright spark, if you'll excuse the pun, invented the percussion cap, a device which replaced gun flints.

Flint has also been extensively used as a building material. The Dolphin Hotel is a good example; the flint was hand-picked for its design.

Gun Cliff is well named, because, in the times when the French threatened invasion, two thirty-pounder cannons were sited on it whilst ten guns were positioned at Beer Head. As this location was more remote, and certainly more exposed to the elements, a hut was erected for the men who manned them. But such is the nature of these cliffs, one night a subsidence took the ten guns and the hut crashing down into the sea. Fortunately, as invasion seemed to be unlikely that night, nobody was on duty!

We finish our brief look at this small fishing village and seaside resort by climbing high into the hills above the village. Pecorama is a tourist attraction, which is well worth a visit by anyone staying in East Devon, but particularly for those folk who like model and miniature railways.

As you will see from the photograph opposite, it was born out of a hilltop open space, when the first sod was cut in 1970. From left to right are: Jim Abraham (Peco sales manager), John Mitchell (works manager), Mrs Cynthia Filbrook (company secretary), Arthur Thorn (Beer Parish Council), Percy Westlake (Chairman of Parish Council), Mr Parsons (digger driver), Sydney Pritchard, Claudine Pritchard and their son Michael.

Peco is the world's leading manufacturer of model railway systems, but, for those who want to experience something a little larger, a ride on the Beer Heights Light Railway, which contours the upper slopes above the village, is superb. Such is the cleverly planned layout that it runs for a mile.

This attraction was officially opened in 1975 by the Revd Wilbert Vere Awdry (1911–1997), the creator of the Thomas the Tank Engine stories. He also blessed and 'christened' the locomotive 'Thomas Junior'. Here he can be seen with his wife Margaret taking a train ride in the first coach. Colin Heard is the train driver. All the children in the village's school were treated to free rides and afternoon tea.

The village was never part of the railway network, but its 'station', Beer Victoria, includes items from former railway stations: awning timbers and valances from Sidmouth; roof tiles from Bridport; the door from the ladies loo at Seaton; and two lamp standards from Bodmin in Cornwall. If you throw in many more items from other stations on the Exeter–Waterloo line, then Beer Victoria can certainly claim to be steeped in railway history!

In addition to all the railway and gardening attractions, there is also a regular programme of entertainments staged in the Garden Theatre.

Pecorama is continually developing, and is a first class tourist attraction with much to offer visitors of all ages. It is free if you are under four, or over eighty years old!

And now we have reached the end of the line, so it must surely be time for a beer: this time, the liquid variety... Cheers!